This book about

Our Father

belongs to

· ·

LION
CHILDREN'S

Jesus liked to pray to God.

Sometimes he went into a room by himself and closed the door. There, alone and quietly, he prayed to God.

Sometimes he got up early
and went for a walk in the
hills. There, alone and quietly,
he prayed to God.

"Teach us to pray," his friends asked him.

"Here is a prayer for always," said Jesus.

Our Father in heaven,

Jesus' followers know they
are all God's children, and
God loves them.

Hallowed be your name,

God's children show respect
for God, because God is
good and holy.

Your kingdom come, your will be done, on earth as in heaven.

God's children remember that God is the real king of the world. They want to do the things that please God.

Give us today our daily bread.

God's children can trust God to take care of them.

Forgive us our sins

Sometimes, God's children do not do what is right. God will forgive them.

As we forgive those who sin against us.

God's children must forgive those who do wrong things to them.

Lead us not into temptation but deliver us from evil.

God's children ask to be kept safe from bad things – the things that make it hard to live as God wants.

They know that God wants to take care of them, as a shepherd takes care of his sheep.

They ask God to hear their prayer.

For the kingdom, the power, and the glory are yours now and for ever. Amen.

Special Words

bread   the food we need

evil   the bad things that spoil the world

hallowed   good and holy

heaven   where God and the angels are

kingdom   the place where a king is in charge

sin   not doing what is right and good

temptation   something that makes it hard to live as God wants

Text by Lois Rock
Illustrations copyright © 2003 Alex Ayliffe
This edition copyright © 2011 Lion Hudson

Published by Lion Children's Books
an imprint of
Lion Hudson plc
Wilkinson House, Jordan Hill Road,
Oxford OX2 8DR, England
www.lionhudson.com/lionchildrens
ISBN 978 0 7459 6314 3
e-ISBN 978 0 7459 6748 6

First edition 2007
This edition 2011

A catalogue record for this book is available from the British Library

Printed and bound in China, May 2014, LH06